FREE VERSE EDITIONS

EDITED BY JON THOMPSON

THEY WHO SAW THE DEEP

GERALDINE MONK

Parlor Press

Anderson, South Carolina

www.parlorpress.com

Parlor Press LLC, Anderson, South Carolina, 29621

Library of Congress Cataloging-in-Publication Data on File

Cover Image: Beach at Morecambe Bay, photograph by Alan Halsey. Used by permission.
Printed on acid-free paper.

Parlor Press, LLC is an independent publisher of scholarly and trade titles in print and multimedia formats. This book is available in paperback and ebook formats from Parlor Press on the World Wide Web at http://www.parlorpress.com or through online and brick-and-mortar bookstores. For submission information or to find out about Parlor Press publications, write to Parlor Press, 3015 Brackenberry Drive, Anderson, South Carolina, 29621, or email editor@parlorpress.com.

Contents

Author's Note

The heart of this book stems from a boat trip on the Libyan Sea in 2014. It was stunningly beautiful but tainted with the inescapable knowledge of the daily death toll of migrants and refugees being lost to its waters. I began to research and write about migration across the seas and down the centuries. The result is the title poem of this book where I interweave lines from ancient Mesopotamian myths.

In the summer of 2015 I was finalising the book in readiness for publication when both these strands became headline news around the world. The first was the intensifying of the refugee crises which swept through Europe and the second was the systematic destruction of the ancient sites in Iraq and Syria culminating in the beheading of the archaeologist and historian Khaled as-Asaad, the eighty-two-year-old keeper of antiquities at Palmyra.

I would therefore like to dedicate this book to the memory of all those who have lost their lives at sea whilst searching for a better life and to Khaled as-Asaad who lost his life whilst protecting the heritage of the world.

– *Geraldine Monk*
August 2015

THEY WHO SAW THE DEEP

How long and careworn
the wanderer must cross,
oar in hand, the rime-cold sea –
the way of outcasts Wyrd leads.

THEY WHO SAW THE DEEP

Viking. North Utsire. South Utsire.

Warning of gales.
Scandinavians.
Westerly. Cyclonic.

Carved snakes malign
horizons. Grizzled North Sea.
Petulant. Tormenting skim of
long ships. Tickling their
underbellies to within an inch.

They came for our wheat.
Wool. Honey. Women.
Tin. Mini-hammers
swinging from their necks.
Kipper ties. *Kiss Me Quick*
etched on their horns.

> *After one league the darkness was*
> *thick and there was no*
> *light. You could see nothing*
> *ahead and nothing*
> *behind.*

I negotiate a monster cauliflower:
pyroclastic flow of the vegetable world.
How come it's so massive?
Is it a drugs cheat? Genetically
modified? I slice distraction.
Outer space deletes light.
An unidentified smell of burning
insinuates malevolence.

I cut my finger on the surprise attack of
longing for unimaginable midsummer
polar mesospheric clouds radiating
false dawns. A pair of fitful atmospheric
doves home in through my kitchen window.

Sea of Nectar Shanty

In the first molecule in the very first molecule.
In the first droplet in the very first droplet.
In the first water in the very first water.
In the very first.
Very.

hydrogen
        oxygen
             sodium
                    chlorine

Forties. Cromarty. Forth. Tyne.

Northerly or northeasterly.
Becoming variable then becoming
southerly or southeasterly. Wintry showers.

From all nautical directions lives held by a
thread of tarred wool. Matted animal hair.
Lashed planks. Bundle rafts.

Isotonic Ocean Water is cryingly
close to our internal body fluids
most notably blood. Hence
diluted Ocean Water aka
Marine Plasma aka Ocean
Plasma aka Marine Serum.

So if we drown in the sea we virtually
drown in ourselves. There is not a crumb
of comfort in this knowledge whatsoever.

> *After two leagues the darkness was*
> *thick and there was no*
> *light. You could see nothing*
> *ahead and nothing*
> *behind.*

What mean Brussels sprouts and
manky too – bad green beads nymph – not
worth the candle. Energy bills.
North Sea Gas.

Is that a whiteout spiking the dark?
Downward penetration of snow.
Orientation disconnects.
Reversed silhouette of
running-on-empty magpie
returns in a deafening temper
putting us all on a knife
edge.

Sea-that-has-become-known Shanty

Nammu Nammu utterly watery deep.
Nammu Nammu chaos of watery deep.
Nammu Nammu void of deep. Gutter of
sweet beneath water. So sweet is.
Very abyss.

bromine
          helium
                  lithium
                          beryllium

Dogger. Fisher. German Bight. Humber.

Rough or very rough.
Rain or thundery showers.
Poor. Occasionally moderate.

Sea tribes threatening.
Angs. Geats. Jutes. Ings.
Sea wolves. Pagans. Pantheists.
Ancestral shades from Doggerland.
Ghosts of no fixed abode.
The world all over at sea.

A time after the island of
Thera blew itself to kingdom
come choking life out the
Aegean
sea people of the deluge
appeared off the coast of
Egypt.
Refugees from Atlantis.
Homeless Minoans. Unnamed
swabbers stiffening into myth.

> *After three leagues the darkness was*
> *thick and there was no*
> *light. You could see nothing*
> *ahead and nothing*
> *behind.*

Brick red sweet potatoes glow
in the encircling gloom.
Edible terracotta. Greased Pyrex
inflamed with love and
wanting. Filthy weather.

Daughter cells cumulate. Propagate
saturation point. Wet bulb potential.
Wren pecks pane over and
over with miniscule distractions of
avian Morse code.

Sea of Fecundity Shanty

Swell of. Swell of.
In the first flesh made fresh made air
made water made original to behold
made her so wondrous she applauded her
down there wondrous waters. Very.

magnesium
        sulphur
                potassium
                        calcium

Thames. Dover. Wight.

Northerly becoming variable.
Rough until later otherwise slight.

Channel rats scuttle intense
depressions along La Manche.
Ocean plasma. TV screens. Booze cruisers.
Below deck bowels heave. Stowaways.
Canned fish teeth. Man meat.
Sardines. Specks of suspended
humanity.

Unfathomable depths.
Recipes for degrees of hurt.
Reduced stock of oxygen. On upper
deck freshly drizzled lemon air.

'Take good care of your sailing cubes and
always make sure your door is safely pulled to'

The above words were written
four thousand years ago. Too late to
save the *Herald of Free Enterprise*.
Most died unseeing in the dark of hypothermia
four soft-boiled minutes from harbour.

> *After four leagues the darkness was*
> *thick and there was no*
> *light. You could see nothing*
> *ahead and nothing*
> *behind.*

The faraway comes near. Sea salt.
Cracked pepper. Surface effort.
Organic granules pour delicious
paradox. Gravy boat. Best china.

Displaced Polar vortex we hear
kindled in fractions love. Snowy owl flying
through a hail of crystal balls. Steering
its monogaze with a hint of uncharacteristic panic.

Sea of Moisture Shanty

Waters of sea devour boat-wolves.
Sea-wolves. Capsized cerulean we
plunge into your oxides.
Deep as the deep blue. Cerulean
we become you. Very.

boron
        carbon
                nitrogen
                        fluorine

Portland. Plymouth.

Cyclonic becoming northwesterly 5 to 6.
Very rough or high. Rain or thundery
showers. Occasionally poor.

When Swiftsure became Speedwell
destined for America it was sabotaged
by a well-worried crew. The Mayflower
stepped up to the plate and did its
legendary bit of ocean ploughing for
sixty five days the Pilgrim Fathers prayed.

A whole month it took to dock unchartered
shores rife with shoal rifts and rock death.
Two lives lost. Oceanus born at sea.
Most died ashore coming to terms with
new vocabularies. Outlandish grave rites.
Beans of many colours. Beyond-fierce weather.

> *After five leagues the darkness was*
> *thick and there was no*
> *light. You could see nothing*
> *ahead and nothing*
> *behind.*

I crumble warm leaves of Greek
sage on turkey. Slices of after-pink
sky appear. Peek-a. Seep-a. Bird calls.
Need a dash of oil.

Robin returned alien-voiced
crackling all night long
destructive notes of great beauty.
Clear air turbulence.
A New England ice storm on the rampage.

Sea of Cleverness Shanty

In the first crumb in the very first crumb.
In the first fig in the very first fig.
In the first come in the very first come.
Deep sweet waters.
Very.

neon
        silicon
                aluminium
                        phosphorous

Biscay. Trafalgar. FitzRoy.

Cyclonic. Occasionally severe gale 9.
Rough or very rough.

Who sails here? Fisher folk. Finisterre a word
haunting itself with end of the earth
all our yesterdays on a loop-tape in the
Wild Bay of the Departed.

What's going down on the event horizon?
A motley crew comes into view with
clinker constructs & papal banners.
Gilded figurehead crafts a bawling infant
blowing poisonous bubbles out its ivory
trumpet spout.

Marauding Normans. Coming for uz
butter-stinkers crouched in ditches
umbles pounding louder than a force
eleven gale awaiting our genocide.
Praying for a storm surge to save our
dark-night soul-sob bacon.

A storm surge did arrive but in 1099 not
1066 the last two digits belly-up and bedevilled.
We were all long gone by then. Dead or
interbred. Women tuk brunt ut latter.

> *After six leagues the darkness was*
> *thick and there was no*
> *light. You could see nothing*
> *ahead and nothing*
> *behind.*

Fine words butter no fish. Parsnips.

Heron cuts a slash across the dusk.
Rheumy-eyed. Bedraggled. A right sorry sight.
Set upon and proper upset. Come home pet. Come home.

Sea of the Edge Shanty

Water stuff of sea struck deep
stern away stern watery boat-lion.
Flood weapon. Carry sweet
deep-weeping boat of all very
heaven. Trawl away.

argon
      scandium
            titanium
                  Vanadium

Sole. Lundy. Fastnet. Irish Sea.

South or Southeast becoming cyclonic.
Wintry showers. Rain or sleet at times.

Sailing again to the Isle of Man for
fresh brown crab on fresh brown bread.
Tender-hearted queenies. Family folk.

In December 1909 the Ellan Vannin vanished in
the unforeseen. All aboard lost. At first light
bags of turnips and an upright piano
boogied up the Mersey. The first bodies
appeared five days later.

> *After seven leagues the darkness was*
> *thick and there was no*
> *light. You could see nothing*
> *ahead and nothing*
> *behind.*

Cat cradles. Baby bones. Tinsel seas.
Milk teeth. Sea seethe. A giant wave of
overwhelm ambushes me in the deep
winter kitchen. It came from nowhere.
I hold a sob at bay draining vitamins.

Hasselback potatoes sprawl well-oiled and
profane against celestial chou-fleur
peppered with tusks of nutmeg.
Meet My Choir on the radio.

Ear-split rattles herald the
return of the jays on the crest of a
squall bulging after dark into
hyperphysical conundrums.

Sea of Showers Shanty

Her heart played reed pipe. His heart
played reed pipe. Animal heart played
reed pipe. Rock hard rock heart played reed pipe.
Five thousand years from home. Five thousand
years of very bones played reed pipe.

chromium

        manganese

                ferrum

                        cobalt

Shannon. Rockall. Malin.

Southerly or southwesterly.
Moderate or rough. Otherwise
very rough or high.

Shannon Boatman is a Canadian footballer
who played for the Toronto Argonauts.
This may be significant but I don't
know why. So I simply present Shannon.
Shannon Boatman and his Argonauts
and let it float.

Treading water. Webbings of fate. In your dreams
a ladder of fine fish bones trundles towards the
smell of doomed stars. Smelling salts. Oil of Vitriol.
Crude bitumen. Spirits queue at the sluice gates.
Recalcitrance of hope.

> *After eight leagues the darkness was*
> *thick and there was no*
> *light. You could see nothing*
> *ahead and nothing*
> *behind.*

SAILING DIRECTIONS FOR THE WORLD:
'If you stand with your back to the
wind in the northern hemisphere the
low pressure lies on your left-hand side'

I stick a fork in the tenderly. Roil of
rare blood guides my precision. Hunger
turns turtle. Warning of gales.

A gust so violent my lungs momentarily
warp. Pulse storm. The swift skims
unseasonable aerobatics. Let me in it cries with
polyhedral notes and out this world mimicry.

Sea of Tranquility Shanty

Isobar brought her mouth close to heaven.
Isotherm brought her mouth close to earth.
Ishtar brought her shroud close to horizon.
Water of life. Coral. Mermaid's purse lips.
Coracle. Sail away. Very away.

nickel
       copperzinc
             gallium
                   germanium

Hebrides. Bailey. Fair Isles.

Northwest gale 8 to storm 10.
High or very high. Poor. Occasionally
very poor.

Decluttering the radar of echoes.
Dissonance. After peace came boat
upon boatload of Vietnamese
bobbing cross black & white
teatime screens. For weeks a
drifting watched without permission
fees or film rights or running water.
Pirates mustered. Moved in. Murdered.
Stole life. Sex. Keepsakes.
Bundled hopes.

> *After nine leagues the darkness was*
> *thick and there was no*
> *light. You could see nothing*
> *ahead and nothing*
> *behind.*

Cloud seeders. Feeder clouds.
Lenticulars. Curly kale is all the rage.
Fat's back. Posh offal. Umbilicals.

An indiscriminate weather bomb bellows.
Wounded bull of heaven. Wheelie bins
never stood a chance. Venetian blinds
skiffle a metal riff. Walls give. Whatever
is happening is happening. Throughout the
land mothers pretend unfear in front of children.

Shepster-starling misread the situation
totally jam-jarred its reflection streaming
glass beads into a ghastly omnishambles
winging a prayer and a hiding to nothing.

Sea of Vapours Shanty

Great above. Heave away. Great below.
Haul away. Dark watery isthmus is.
Swags of cedarwood. Overlays. Her
apple fresh was wondrous. Precious lapis.
Fragrant boxwood. Amber oud.

arsenic
       selenium
              krypton
                    rubidium

Faeroes. Southeast Iceland.

Westerly 3 or 4, backing northerly 6 to
gale 8. Very rough or high. Snow showers.
Good, occasionally poor.

Colossal displacements of cloud clusters.
The fearful & forsook set sail on death
ships. Nightly ebb and flow of nascent
diasporas listing in the wake of good ship
Tye the Triton from Iceland patrolling this *'pig of a sea'.*

It's very low key this World War Three.
Not declared just accumulated conflicts.
Pathological structural remodelling of hearts
traverse the Mare Nostrum from Syria. Afghanistan.
Libya. Bangladesh. Nigeria. Mali. Somalia. Eritrea. Et...

Many arrive in new shoes. If they arrive. Survive
abandonment. Junk freights. Animal folds.
Scuttlings. Two-faced faceless crews. Masked
amputations. Dehydration. Desponds. Exposure.
Hungry waves. Requiem sharks.

> *After ten leagues the darkness was*
> *thick and there was no*
> *light. You could see nothing*
> *ahead and nothing*
> *behind.*

Seabed sunken cities tenderly catch the daily
fall of new inhabitants. Lampedusa awaits its
loggerhead turtles. Deeply meandering jet
stream. An inconsolable fog of steam rises
from the almost-ready Sunday lunch.

Old Saharan air. A Spanish Plume rents
asunder. Severe atmospheric underbellies.
Doves have had enough. They perform a no show.
That's it. Dishing up.

Sea of Crises Shanty

Shattered the churn shattered the cup.
Shattered the junk shattered the ocean-going.
In the first water in the very first water.
In the first droplet in the very first droplet.
In the first molecule in the very first molecule.
In the very first.

strontium
        yttrium
                zirconium
                        niobium

Coda

If I rise on the wings of dawn, if I settle on the far side of the sea.

If I ride the wings of morning, if I dwell by the farthest oceans.

If I take the wings of the morning and dwell in the uttermost parts of the sea.

If I take the wings of the morning *and* dwell in the uttermost parts of the sea.

If I live at the eastern horizon or settle at the western limits.

If I take wings with the dawn and settle down on the western horizon.

If I were to fly on the wings of the dawn, and settle down on the other side of the sea.

If I shall lift my wings like an Eagle's and dwell at the end of the Sea.

If I take the wings of the dawn and dwell in the uttermost parts of the sea.

If I take the wings of the morning, and dwell in the uttermost parts of the sea.

If I take wings early in the morning, and dwell in the uttermost parts of the sea.

(If) I take the wings of the dawn (and) dwell in the uttermost parts of the sea.

If I take the wings of the dawn, and settle in the uttermost parts of the sea.

If I climb upward on the rays of the morning sun or land on the most distant shore of the sea where the sun sets.

If I take the wings of the morning. If I were to speed across the earth on the wings of the dawn, and, having done so, were to dwell in the uttermost parts of the sea.

If I take the wings of the morning...and fly as swift as the morning light to east, to the extremity of it...and dwell in the uttermost parts of the sea; in the most distant isles of it, in the farthest parts of the world.

I take the wing of morning, I dwell in the uttermost part of the sea.

DELIQUIUM

Four Definitions Between Crete and Canterbury

(chemistry)

Liquefaction
through absorption of
moisture from the air.

Un-northern will have to do
as nothing compares to your
division of blue so clenched
it hurts this
Libyan sea's
invasive depth
so far flung from all
accumulated waters I have

seen

horizons tooth-spooked
heavy breathing
waves
molest my
exposed back
against the sun
long pork
over salted
scratching
melanoma

bother

other plots and
growths
maligning
iron oxide forms
a bed for Becket's
hallowed
brim o' lice.

(pathology)

An abrupt loss of
consciousness usually
caused by an insufficient
blood flow to the brain:
fainting.

Excommunication of the self.

Sunstruck. Heatstroke. Upshot.

His blood
white with brain his
brain no less red with blood
a dying a cathedral a floored
mosaic forever and a lasting
age her arms raised aloft
two birds
balance her Cretan crown
with wit her decorated
breasts sit where
breasts sit being geometric
and loudly unapologetic.

We sit out on our transient
balcony avoiding a battalion of
testy spikes. Trying to cram down
emergency room service club
sandwiches too massive for
our bemused bouches.

How on earth do you
eat a butty these
days as fat as a ram's
bottom and who
will rid us of
this turbulent
feast a requiem
dangling
blue as uncooked
steak in
Canterbury.

(literary)

A languid, maudlin mood.

Duck-egg.
Moon-fool.
Rubble of love
shattered across the
vaulted heaven help
us my posing painted
hot-goddess –
oh god she's not amused –
gisuz a-kiss my stern
lovely miss
worse things happen at
sea surf-riders
drunk with vertigoing
riptides hanging on for
dear irresistible
death-drag.

Show me the days to go home.

There are more seabirds in landlocked
Sheffield than on the coast of Crete.
More waterspouts in Canterbury
honed by our stonemasons
bestowing our nowadays
with lucrative
heritage.

Souls of gurning gargoyles circle. Ingest.

Gisuz-a-hug luv
for crying out steeped in
stone shredding half a
head in a right bit of
bad butchery
beneath the
cankered
cantering
stars.

(rare)

An abrupt absence of sunlight
e.g. caused by an eclipse.

Malfeasance in office.
Occulted vision.

Put out the light and
then put out the
extraordinary
fight against
sudden dips into

where the hell am I?

Birds cease their
territorial
bicker-bicker
so-called songs.

Getting back to
malfeasance
occulted vision –
intolerance is all the
rage now everyone
owns fury within
three steps to heaven
hexes tossed
in the manner of
confetti flutter.
Heart stopover.
Temperature drop.

*'The night has a thousand eyes
and the day but one'*

Hot yogurt
tart. Stone cold
pudding.
Walnuts on
ice.

Coda

Gathers the waters of the sea into jars: puts the deep into storehouses.

Assigned the sea its boundaries and locked the oceans in vast reservoirs.

Gathers the oceans in a single place; put the deep water into storehouses.

Piles up the water of the sea; puts the oceans in storehouses.

Gathers the water in the sea like a dam and puts the oceans in storehouses.

Gathers the waters of the sea as a heap; puts the deeps in storehouses.

Gathers the waters of the sea together as a heap; lays up the deeps in
storehouses.

Gathers the waters of the sea into a heap; puts the depths into storehouses.

Gathered the waters of the seas like water skins and set the deep in
storehouses.

Piles up the water of the sea; puts the oceans in storehouses.

Gathereth the waters of the sea together as a heap; layeth up the deeps in
store-houses.

Gathering together the waters of the seas as in a vessel, laying up the depths
in storehouses.

Gathers the waters of the sea together as a heap. Lays up the deeps in
storehouses.

Gathering as a heap the waters of the sea. Putting in treasuries the depths.

THE ABANDONED

The Snake Goddess of Crete

I cannot grasp your high status apron
(your pretty little pinny) in my hands to
blow my nose and wipe my eyes as
of a child of yours and wash away this
here-now world and find a maybe
kinder variant. It's like this you see –
I don't much care for the 21ˢᵗ century.

The uproar of many peoples who roar
roaring seas rumbling of nations
rushing on rumble of waters roaring mighty
uproar of many peoples who roar seas
rumbling of nations grumbling mighty
roar of seas of nations of up roaring.

I need to touch your transfixed snakes.
Stroke the sejant cat perched on your crown
and suck your startling tits as of a babe
wash away this here-now world to find a
kinder crew. To sail our tabernacle divine
with fearless balance at your fingertips.

Artemis Comes to Tea

The lacuna of the afternoon
tempts apparitions
in stop-gaps of space.
Vinegar flies or motes or
floaters in my eyes
construct the middle
distance show –
atomic baubles of
lo-salt spray-on no-fat.

With a sigh I excavate my spectacles.

Food must be prepared for rare visitations.
Artemis of Ephesus will beam through
my inner kitchen door her unblinking
orbs fierce with unseeing.

Here she comes!

Rivers of goats and griffins preening
        breasts
bee eggs
                leopard breath
horny things
        electric claws
lion wings all creatures great &
small gully down her teeming
pleats and plaits.

I examine the fare – would she prefer
pomegranates
                    blue cheese
            green
        tea
time assorted biscuits – bull's testicles?

I close the door gently and
pray like a mantis.

Freya's Torque

Uber-imps and boss drags. Rows of grotesques
stud Lincoln Cathedral. One spoiling for a fight
face wedged like a bruise in the wood so real I could
smell its fetid breath. Our eyes locked. A heartbeat away
from recognition. Filaments turned in my spine canal.
Mutual suspicion was profound. Getting personal.

Tumbling out the cloisters in a messy medieval
kind of way we fell into a Christmas market
earnestly being Christmassy. Cheap cheerful
crafts. Mince pies. Meads. Lancashire cheese
bombs. Soft fruit targets. Leg-weary. Winter-
weary. A little dispirited. And then I saw her.

Love. Sex. Death. War. Beauty. Wrapped in a cloak of
falcon feathers. Two cats to pull her. A wild boar by
her side. Round her neck the Brisingamen torque.
Round my neck Freya. Unsought goddess shining
in the dismal light. Tiny as a one pound coin.

Juno Luna & Alanus
(Duet from Midsummer Mummery*)*

. . . my uprisings	planets
reverse	shooting
thing-things	thing-things
my solar winds	bones-with
stain Earth	blood things
rain	with-skin
sky	I glow you
green to violet	I grow 386
sways	billion billion
shudder-heft	megawatts of
light show	shows

> *spin*
> *spin*
> *counter-spin*
> *counter-spin*
> *helium spin*
> *helium spin*
> *hydrogen*
> *hydrogen*
> *shine-on*
> *shine-on*
> *gamma*
> *gamma*
> *(gamma)*   *(gamma)*
> *rays*
> *rays*
> *nuke fission-vision*
> *nuke fission-vision*
> *rotate my*
> *rotate my*
>
> *core*

Orante Chants

You have good taste she shouts at my
back as I exit the shop and scamper over
breakneck cobbles into the shadow of gulls.

What a corker. A squat & fierce female
sporting a no-mess-monobrow
wrestling under my armpit chanting
mantras through the bubble wrap.
They who go down to the sea in
ships have seen her standing there.
Listen deep:

...Straight things. Pulling things. Sending things
away. Things shaking. Things like water.
Moist things. Drying things up things. Things
like the sea. Things like snakes. Touching holy
things. Hot things. Burning things. Hearing things.
Not seeing spirit things...

She incants the universe so outlandishly off-key
sea sponges deconstruct without hope of reformation.

Orante Flies Home

My psychic exoskeleton was in turmoil.
The inner-sea crashing madly for home.
Worn out with prickly heat and lights in harbour
caught fast in the faraway, the heart taps a
doleful rhythm against its cage. Vision fails.
My eye changes shape and swarms with Optrex.

Back home I unpack the wailing bubble wrap.
The content emerges like a ship's anchor. Arms
aloft. Head locked. Cast iron stare. A tattooed beard
on her chin. She has turned truculent under the
weight of northern skies. She is still chanting:

...Invisible things. Seeking concrete things.
Seeking abstract things. Uncertain things.
Deceptive things. Things wearing out. Existence
of things. Killing animal things. Things passing away.
Things stuck together. All things being possible
things. Things happening. Things not remotely.
Crazed orbits of things...

Hers is the day. Hers is the night.

I place her gently
on a shelf with
Others.

The sun knows the place of its setting.

United Female Animates

Ishtar Artemis Nammu Astarte
Minerva Isis Athena Nanab Hecate
Ashtaroth Inanna Maryam Lilith
Eve Absusu et al. set out with their
screech-owls wild-dogs steed-boars
body-snakes raptors love-doves
crown-perching cats skirt-bees
lion-wings et al.

An unholy crew with their fabulous
familiars combined forces and swaggered
down the crooked-paths spooked-crossed roads
wild-hills watery-deeps airy-waves
highways & mean city streets. Bows & arrows &
spears & animals primed for action. They
stormed *The Cock and Bull* and had the
mother-of-all girls' nights out.
Partied till the dawn of time.

Coda

Who shut up the sea behind doors when it burst forth from the womb.

Who kept the sea inside its boundaries as it burst from the womb.

Or who shut in the sea with doors when it burst out from the womb.

Or who enclosed the sea with doors When, bursting forth, it went out from the womb.

Or *who* shut up the sea with doors, when it brake forth, as *if* it had issued out of the womb?

Who enclosed the sea behind doors when it burst from the womb.

Who enclosed the sea with limits when it gushed out of the womb.

Who shut up the sea with doors when it burst forth, coming out of the womb.

Who shut the sea behind gates when it burst through and came out of the womb.

Or who shut up the sea with doors, when it broke forth, as if it had issued out of the womb.

Or who shut up the sea with doors, when it broke forth, as it had issued out of the womb;

Who shut up the sea with doors, when it broke forth as issuing out of the womb:

And who shut up the sea with doors, when it broke forth, issuing out of the womb?

THE BAY AREA

The Bay

This may be the place Ptolemy dubbed
'Morikambe' between the rivers
Ribble and Solway. Or it may not.
Morecambe Bay in the county of Lancashire
is not strictly a bay but a multiple estuary. A
thing of lucid beauty. A thing of light-spawned
shimmers. Hefted waters. Gravid daubs.
Bits of seethe and brood. A bent sea.
A crooked bay. A serial killer.

> *The really bored lad dragged his face from the screen*
> *just long enough to pass our room key. The only*
> *inhabitant we'd seen since check-in. A high season*
> *seafront hotel abandoned to vacancy. Unverified shades.*

Uplift of heart-cockles brim with abstraction.
Salt flats. Mud flats. Sand banks. Quick sands.
The largest intertidal flats in Britain.
Shallow sub-tidal sands. Tide-washed channels.
Shingle spits. Skears. Skerries. Insinuations.
Sibylline loops of calligraphy. Five tidal bores leave
calling cards across the bay. They will deviate.
Tease. Render evidence untraceable.

> *An obscure foreboding feathered our shoulders.*
> *In the deserted dining room a flotilla of napkins*
> *sailed in the half-dark stiff with untouched*
> *attitudes. Unblemished.*

The sea was out. Way beyond God's back
out. Doing its end-of-pier vanishing act.
Somewhere out there five tidal bores loosening
up. Oiling roars. Flexing oxygenated muscles.
Mobilising hydrogen. Combined forces gathering
obscene amounts of protein. Let's name names:
Leven. Kear. Kent Wyre. Lune.

Dangerous texts spike the coastline:

BEWARE!
SHIFTY CHARACTERS. TERRA-SLIPS
HOODED CHANNELS. FIVE GO MAD
MEDUSA COMPLEX
POTTED-SHRIMP-THINGS
LOOSE LEAF SEA FOG. FEET GRABBERS
NABBERS. SOUL SNATCHERS

Submarine swards of smart red fescue, thrift and
plantain. The muffled thrum of trembling sea mats.
Short-snouted sea horses. Phosphorescent Sea Pens.
Free-wheeling crustaceans. Phantoms from the glacial
relic of the Lune Deep. All life begat and spat teeming.

> We mount incrementally unlit stairs.
> Scrabble for landing lights. Wade through
> troughs. Corridors. Reek of stewed sea-cabbage
> leached from air vents. Sulphuric. Sixth sense on
> full alert. Lugworms. Zooplankton. Real-time dread.

Incoming tides can outrun a man. A spooked horse.
Shortcut chancers. Long-legged children. Economic
migrants. From nothing to neck-deep in minutes. From
quick blood to clarty corpse the salt & vinegar air fills up.
Melancholy lodges between teeth, darkens the living daylights.

> Our room was cellular. Deeply dingy. Forlorn
> pillows. Lumpy bed. No soap. Dialled O for reception
> got a monotonic sea drone. Freak wave. Mobile also
> dead. Outside the door a squall of shocking laughter.
> After midnight runners. We make makeshift barricades.
> Curl-up childish and close. In fitful sleep I proffer a
> disheartened cheek to a no-kiss.
> The sea grew.

The Lune Deep is a marine canyon running from
Fleetwood to The Bay. Ice age scar tissue. Miles of
deep throat vertiginous reef cliffs. Tumbledown flora.
Configurations with eyes. Spiracles.
A wonderworld beneath our wonderworld.

We begin the descent to the breakfast room.
Hope sinks without trace. Shrouds of white linen
draped everywhere. We find a small clearing of
orange Formica set for two. We sit and wait. And wait.
Nobody comes. Radio babble drifts through frosted
glass. We enter the kitchen. Our hunger is greeted by old
bacon smells. Rolling news. Piles of raw chicken. Uncooked eggs.
We shout for service. Shout at the top of our lungs.

Lune

(For my great-great grandfather Christopher Reed)

The slippage was between rivers and time.

Driving through the undulations of the Trough of
Bowland a preternatural light skulked withershins.
The Bay beyond redemption came into view on our
left. The Faraway mumbling...oh never mind.

Veering inland to Arkholme the old family farm
still there. Still a farm. Fields so familiar they crashed
my DNA. It seriously wasn't ours anymore. We built it in
1709. Lost a century later. Blame laws against women.
Mortality. The draw of short straws.

Taking the road down to the river we stall outside
Ferryman's Cottage from where my ancestors
departed. Their last earthly journey was to sail across
this river. Rowed in rustic coffins across the Lune to Melling.
Obolus dead weights ballast their eyes. Winding sheets.
Paddled to the last by Keen-gaze. Death carrier. Tom Charon.

That day the river was brackish in parts. Abstruse.
A slick so dense a black it sucked all light from your eyes.
Drank your breath out. Oil of extreme unction. Oesophagus.
Sarcophagus. Loyn. River of Pain. River of Wailing.
River of Forgetfulness. River of Flaming. River of
Detestation. Five rivers of death. Five tidal bores.

River of Homecoming.

On a sandbank I almost see someone
tragic with a crooked nose and a
missing finger. He crashes my DNA.
Was this the sandbank we owned?
Could this be...oh never mind.

Voyage
(35 years returning)

I am jettisoned on an artery cut cockerel screama shock of
mercury staining red this sanguineous vessel full of float and
buoyanting on wavery knots then blistered and besieged by
time ticking creatures rubbing heataway the seconds and
the haw-haw raw and caustic figures and the dreary moments
fall-in-slow-in-motion avoiding flash laughing burnout
stilted dark flamingo pink and neck-humped sore and softly
catching this speck and that fickle shard and somewhere hide
those grey and brilliant rooms where hunting radars clamp and
spear trackindown trackindown crackindown the quarry.

Now the hungry the bloated floating easy as clouds
butting putrid fables shutting gin traps on slender ankles
time goes toothless and dull a thickening paste with a
sickening taste to rhyme and with nothing to lean on
but a pale afternoon I will abandon this ship.

Coda

By the blast of her nostrils the waters piled up. The surging waters stood up like a wall: the deep waters congealed in the heart of the sea.

At the blast of her breath, the waters piled up! The surging waters stood straight like a wall; in the heart of the sea the waters became hard.

At the blast of her nostrils the waters piled up; the floods stood up in a heap; the deeps congealed in the heart of the sea.

And with the blast of her nostrils the waters were gathered together, the floods stood upright as a heap, *and* the depths were congealed in the heart of the sea.

The waters heaped up a blast of Her nostrils; the currents stood firm like a dam. The watery depths congealed in the heart of the sea.

By the breath of her nostrils the waters were piled up, the flowing waters stood up like a hill, the deep waters congealed in the heart of the sea.

By the blast of her nostrils the waters were piled up, the flowing water stood upright like a heap, and the deep waters were solidified in the heart of the sea.

With the blast from her nostrils, the water piled up. The waves stood up like a dam. The deep water thickened in the middle of the sea.

And with the blast of her nostrils the waters were gathered together, the floods stood upright as a heap, and the depths were congealed in the heart of the sea.

And with the blast of her anger the waters were gathered together; the flowing water stood, the depths were gathered together in the midst of the sea.

And by the breath of her nostrils the waters were heaped up; The streams stood as a mound; The depths were congealed in the heart of the sea.

With the blast of her nostrils the waters were gathered together.

THREE VERSIONS OF THREE SHIPS

For Bill Griffiths

One

You were
and always will be
my first friend in
this
our
shadowy
Word World &
Darker Dictionary.

No Wonder we loved ghosts hiding
out in the hinterland or
stumbling along these biting shores
spooning fossils from their salt-steep
marinated longer
than our minds could stretch the
deep-North Sea-horizons
orisons –

Who learned our carol and carried it away.
I saw three ships so beautiful and small
so delicate and tall and bought them all
to come sailing in on every day
in the morning-lands of your rooms.
The full yeast swell ova bowl ov bread
– if we had only conquer'd the air.

A leap down of apples

When mobile life rages off
into space, a little handke
rchief or two of budding co
tton will give a tremble.

                    Fo
                    xes astray in the stars.
                    That there are always other po
                    wers: that they are gaps
                    moonless to lie with a million
                    stars vibrating & talking a
                    bove (you) communicating by
                    colour some by the fierce in
                    gredients ov their flicker
                    ing tolling...

                                                        La
                                                        nd-awake on a tiny
                                                        pivot of
                                                        love.

For (you) are sweetness all thru like
brown bananas, transparent b
ruises, & (you) link word & memory
along
cradling a(nother) tiny model boat
(in the glow of)
the fragile arc our light moves in.

Two

You were
and always will be   my first friend in & (you)
link word & memory
this

              along
our
cradling a (nother) tiny model **boat**
shadowy

(in the glow of)

Word World &
the fragile arc our light moves **in**.
Darker Dictionary.
For (you) are sweetness all **thru** like.

No wonder we loved ghosts hiding
                    out in the hinterland or
La
stumbling along these biting shores
nd
awake on a tiny pivot of   spooning
fossils from their salt-steep
love
marinated longer
        than our minds could stretch the

deep-North Sea-horizons

orisons –

That there are always other po
wers: that they are **gaps**.

Who learned our carol and carried it away   moonless
to lie with a million

stars vibrating & talking a
bove **(you)** communicating by

col**our** some by the fierce in
gredients ov their flicker

ing tolling...
                             I saw three ships so beautiful and small
so delicate and tall and bought them all
                                  to come sailing in
on every day
xes astray in the stars
in the morning-lands of your rooms.

The full yeast swell ova bowl ov **bread**
 – if we had only conquer'd the **air**

When mobile life rages off

into space, a little handke.
A leap down of apples.

Chief or two of budding co
tton will give a
tremble.

Three

In moves light our arc fragile
(in the glow of)
model boat tine a(nother) cradling
along memory & word link (you) &
transparent banana brown like thru
all sweetness are (you) for.

Love
of pivot tiny on awake
land.

tolling...
flicker their ingredients
in fierce colour by
communicating (you) a
bove talking & vibrating
stars a million lie moonless
gaps are they powers.
Other always are there.

Stars in the astray.
Foxes.

Tremble a cotton
budding two
handkerchief
s
pace off rages life
mobile.

Apples of down
leap a.

Air conquer'd bread
bowl swell yeast full.

Rooms your
morning-lands in the
every day sailing
come them all so delicate
and tall
small and beautiful
ships
three I saw.

Who learned our carol and carried it away?

Orisons.
Sea-horizons.
North-deep the stretch
our minds longer marinated
salt-steep their fossils
spooning
shores biting
stumbling
hinterland out in the
hiding ghosts we loved
wonder.

Dictionary darker
&
World word
shadowy
our
this friend
first will
always.

SOME SHIPS SMELT VIVIDLY OF FISH

The Forgotten War – Korea 1950-1953

They said the whole country
stank of human shit. Three years
later the whole country stank of
human blood. Both are problematic
but excellent fertilizers.

He broke off mid-mind-reel
macular-gaze skimming
over my head obliterating
my self-conscious goon face.
He slid down his Korean
foxhole into everlasting
purgatory. The troop ships
had taken weeks to reach the
unforgettable. Time out for
clowning. Browning knees.

He pointed to his punitive cancer.
Another old soldier eaten up
with guilt. I'd met so many from
all last century's wars. He won't go
further into this...his abyss...
his killing fields.

It was the jaw-locking cold he spoke of most
sidestepping freshly dead bodies. During
the night in their dugouts their overcoats froze
solid. They huddled. Smoked ciggies for warmth.
He half-laughed...*it was rotten...*.

After the A-bomb and H-Bomb after Hiroshima and
Nagasaki war would never be the same and for almost
twenty four hour it wasn't. On August 10th 1945
America agreed to occupy Korea. By 1950 occupation
bloated into war. Zero to the bone war.
Dislocating. Hand-to-hand.
Bad-hot-breath. Death-necking combat.
Sludge-baths. Torture larks.

Distinguishing signals from noise. That's
the key. Boys will be boys but men were
scared stiff bugging-out all over the show.
So ill-trained many blew their brains out
trying to work their which-way-up weapons.

Everything was dammed & jammed & frozen.

He was back talking cold. Language splintered
when he tried to speak. The exhaustion of inescapable
memory. Then one day and forty five years on the
monkey jumped.

...It was kill or be killed...

After the revelation the dinner was served. Meat
and two veg. Treacle pudding. Afternoon bingo.
His seeing eyes imprinted on the ceiling.

Across the sea the ghosts of
split atoms glowed. After the second
strike another light. Never the third.
Goodnight...

Irene goodnight... Irene goodnight...
Goodnight Irene...goodnight Irene...
I'll see you in my dreams...

REBOUNDS

Trouvé

Under my grubby fingernails
micro-tropes grow interpretations in
half moon rows. Rune compost.
Organisms grin their toothy patterns beneath
accusations of bright crimes never
committed.

DNA. The atomic bomb. Carbon dating. Our Blue Marble
Planet. New dimensions exfoliate astonished psyches.
Metempsychosis of sin inches free with each excavation.
Daughters of Eve damned to the abyss of myth
make a mad dash. Staggering massive. Survivors. Sunder
cores.

Neanderthal genome roams through our modern
bones. Retrovirus telling tales. Unearthing
dirt of innocence. Protean rocks.
Fundamental traceries.
Blush of folding
globins.

...brave new worlds quake in the wake of rude horizons...

Rock-a-Bye

Product: *Synthetic diamonds*
created from the remains of humans.

That must anger angels and cacodemons.
I hear them now slashing crossed wings
in an almighty strop.

Repositories of nuance diminish.
Unevolving stockpiles of images,
corrupt memory,
electronic voice deception.
Codicils.
A lock of hair.

How to outsmart entropy. Immutability.

Qi.   Pneuma.   Prana.

In Hassocks near the garden centre
corpses are baked into submission.
Dust beyond dust purified carbon
mutates into a dazzler.
'It can take up to nine months'
From embryo to eternity the
ultimate done deal
ousts our sulking ghosts as
death swaggers its bling.

Sweetheart. Shall we shell our souls?
Cut them to facets. Make light our eternal
playmate. A drop of you or me could nest
near our heart or beneath the long night
pillow but when we both depart do
we end up on Ebay to be pawed by
strangers in perpetuity.

Prana.   Pneuma.   Qi.

The Eyes Have It

To resist the mystical is
easier when having a
face-off with a rodent in the
barefooted early hours on the
kitchen floor than having a
face-to-face with a big cat behind
manicured bars in a zoo.
Not all gazes are equal.
The owl and the pussy cat grapple
our wandering souls to a standstill of
supernatural awe. The rat and the
bunny rabbit not quite so.

When the drunk kissed the Rottweiler in the chippy
it took half his face off with reciprocal passion.

WHERE THE NINE LADIES AREN'T

(Co-authored with Alan Halsey for performance by two voices)

From an unclassified road
Hulleys service to Stanton in Peak
Tom Tom download
5 miles SE of Bakewell

Shallow Grange – Farditch –
Nether Low – Great Low –
Hillhead – Hind Low –
Hatch-a-Way –

Jericho –

Stoop Farm – Red Hurst –
Greensides – Fox Low –
Back Dale – Diamond Hill –
Cliff Farm – The

Frith –

Bumper Castle – Cow Close –
Eagle Tor – Hillcarr –
Hollow Farm – Clough Wood –
Hermit's Cape – Robin Hood's

S-t-r-i-d-e –

Just a 20 minute walk
from Black Fly Layby
says the friendly dustyhaired
stumbling drystonewaller

pointing vaguely to the upper abyss

in the dark lanes of Derbyshire
meandering aimless unknowing
if it's a different thing we haven't found.

I take issue with this issue of
so-called ladies stoned to death eternal
dancing on our common heaths
transgressing unconceived
anachronistic Sabbaths.

There are ten stones but only nine ladies

So who is the tenth that danceth besides us
the fiddler no doubt – he's always cast as a
clout-eared fool in thrall to lesser.

perhaps because one of the stones is apparently invisible

invisibly apparent

or as some say the tenth only emerged

you mean the wicked male musician?

from the formerly grassed-over rubble bank

you mean the wicked male musician

during the drought of '76.
Another discovered three years later.
The ladies were turned to stone
as a penalty for
sorry
some of the content is not available
please try later.

DANCING!

Possibly the Bronze Age inhabitants also thought
that Stanton Moor is in a fine position
overlooking the Derwent and Wye valleys.

Possibly the Bronze Age inhabitants thought
the view was secondary to being eaten alive by black fly
wild boar or every other hungry tribe within
spitting-dist.

Despite the complete lack of archaeological evidence

    complete lack
and recent
      recent
planting of a small copse
        planting of a small copse
obscuring the view
      obscuring view
but once
    once
they also
    also
recently planted
     planted wild
wild grasses
    wild wild grasses
flowers
    wers
start seeding themselves
     seeding them
the place will look a lot
     will look a lot
more natural
    natural.

Oh so go-go unnatural ladies.

Don't go expecting anything on the scale of
for example Stonehenge.

Or as commercial.

There are pagans who think
that other pagans' offerings are litter.

bugbugbugbugbugbugbug
    bugbugbugbugbugbugbug

Vandals have recently dabbed
    daubed
dabdabadaub
    dabdabadaub

green and yellow paint on all the ladies

Painted ladies.

Every lady must get stoned.

Newly scattered ashes
somebody's remains but
do not try to clean the paint off
it is criminal evidence
and you may be viewing
yesterday's version of this
page. *Yesterday...*

    all our versions seemed so far away

Wood	Low	Ditch	Sides	Cape
Eagle	Robin	Stoop	Green	
Shallow	Hermit	Hollow	Farm	Fox
Jericho	Hill	Frith	Clough	
Head	Bumper	Hood	Nether	Stride
Red	Diamond	Carr	Tor	
Close	Cow	Far	Dale	Back
Cliff	Great	Castle	Hurst	
Way	Hatch	Hind	Grange	Away

Acknowledgments

The epigraph is an adaptation by Alan Halsey and Geraldine Monk from the Anglo-Saxon text *The Wanderer.*

Magazines and anthologies: *Poetry Wales, Long Poem Magazine, Golden Handcuffs Review, Litmus, The Animal Gaze, Drifting Down the Lane, Black-box Manifold, past simple.*

'Midsummer Mummery': the full version was written for performance by the antichoir *Juxtavoices.*

'Where The Nine Ladies Aren't' was co-authored with Alan Halsey and performed for S.J. Fowlers' *Camaradfest II.*

Special Thanks

To my sister-in-law Janet Monk for her tireless research into our family tree especially in regard to the poem "Lune" which is dedicated to my great-great grandfather Christopher Reed who being dispossessed of his farm and livelihood in his 50's died in prison for the crime of trying to keep alive.

Notes on Texts

THEY WHO SAW THE DEEP

The shipping forecasts are all taken from the British Maritime and Coastguard Agency reports in December 2014.

Several sources were used for the translations of the Sumerian myths and legends. I predominantly draw on the Sumerian Creation Myth, the texts of Inanna (Ishtar), The Epic of Gilgamesh and the pre-biblical narratives of the Great Flood or Deluge. Allusions and references to these myths appear elsewhere in the book.

CODAS

These are adapted from variants of biblical texts.

DELIQUIUM

'The night has a thousand eyes' is from a poem of that name by Francis William Bourdillion.

VOYAGE is taken from the last section of a poem I wrote in 1979 which was published in *Spreading the Cards,* Siren Press, 1980.

SOME SHIPS SMELT VIVIDLY OF FISH

The title and factual information was taken from *The Korean War* by Max Hastings, Michael Joseph, 1987.

About the Author

Geraldine Monk's poetry was first published in the 1970s and has appeared in countless magazines and anthologies. Her main collections include *Interregnum* (Creation Books) and *Escafeld Hangings* (West House Books). *The Salt Companion to Geraldine Monk* edited by Scott Thurston appeared in 2007, and in 2012 she edited the collective autobiography of selected British poets in *Cusp: Recollections of Poetry in Transition* (Shearman Books). She is an affiliated poet at the Centre of Poetry and Poetics at The University of Sheffield, U.K.

Free Verse Editions

Edited by Jon Thompson

13 ways of happily by Emily Carr
Between the Twilight and the Sky by Jennie Neighbors
Blood Orbits by Ger Killeen
The Bodies by Chris Sindt
The Book of Isaac by Aidan Semmens
Canticle of the Night Path by Jennifer Atkinson
Child in the Road by Cindy Savett
Condominium of the Flesh by Valerio Magrelli, trans. by Clarissa Botsford
Contrapuntal by Christopher Kondrich
Country Album by James Capozzi
The Curiosities by Brittany Perham
Current by Lisa Fishman
Dismantling the Angel by Eric Pankey
Divination Machine by F. Daniel Rzicznek
Erros by Morgan Lucas Schuldt
The Forever Notes by Ethel Rackin
The Flying House by Dawn-Michelle Baude
Instances: Selected Poems by Jeongrye Choi, translated by Brenda Hillman, Wayne de Fremery, & Jeongrye Choi
The Magnetic Brackets by Jesús Losada, translated by Michael Smith & Luis Ingelmo
A Map of Faring by Peter Riley
No Shape Bends the River So Long by Monica Berlin & Beth Marzoni
Pilgrimly by Siobhán Scarry
Physis by Nicolas Pesque, translated by Cole Swensen
Poems from above the Hill & Selected Work by Ashur Etwebi, translated by Brenda Hillman & Diallah Haidar
The Prison Poems by Miguel Hernández, translated by Michael Smith
Puppet Wardrobe by Daniel Tiffany
Quarry by Carolyn Guinzio
remanence by Boyer Rickel
Signs Following by Ger Killeen
Split the Crow by Sarah Sousa
Spine by Carolyn Guinzio
Spool by Matthew Cooperman
Summoned by Guillevic, translated by Monique Chefdor & Stella Harvey
Sunshine Wound by L. S. Klatt

These Beautiful Limits by Thomas Lisk
They Who Saw the Deep by Geraldine Monk
The Thinking Eye by Jennifer Atkinson
An Unchanging Blue: Selected Poems 1962–1975 by Rolf Dieter Brinkmann,
    translated by Mark Terrill
Under the Quick by Molly Bendall
Verge by Morgan Lucas Schuldt
The Wash by Adam Clay
We'll See by George Godeau, translated by Kathleen McGookey
What Stillness Illuminated by Yermiyahu Ahron Taub
Winter Journey [Viaggio d'inverno] by Attilio Bertolucci, translated by
    Nicholas Benson
Wonder Rooms by Allison Funk

www.ingramcontent.com/pod-product-compliance
Lightning Source LLC
Chambersburg PA
CBHW022037090426
42741CB00007B/1100